Los Molinos

The Windmills

(...and other Selected Translated Poetry, of: Juan Parra del Riego)

Selections of Juan Parra del Riego: Chosen, Edited, and Translated by Dr. Dennis L. Siluk Ed. D.
Three Time Poet Laureate (& Rosa Peñaloza de Siluk)

In English and Spanish

The Council (ruling body) of the Continental University, of Huancayo, Peru, congratulates and recognizes Dr. Dennis Lee Siluk for his abundant intellectual contribution (with his writings), permitting the Mantaro Valley's attributes to be known worldwide. November, 27, 2008

iUniverse®

THE WINDMILLS (LOS MOLINOS)
...AND OTHER SELECTED TRANSLATED POETRY, OF: JUAN PARRA DEL RIEGO

Front cover illustration by Dennis L. Siluk (2007)
Juan Parra del Riego, in Montevideo

All translations were done by Rosa Peñaloza de Siluk, and edited by
The author, Dennis L. Siluk

Picture on back of book of the author at the Barnes and Nobel bookstore, in
Har Mar Mall, Roseville, Minnesota doing a book signing in February 2006.

iUniverse books may be ordered through booksellers or by contacting:

iUniverse
1663 Liberty Drive
Bloomington, IN 47403
www.iuniverse.com
844-349-9409

ISBN: 978-1-4401-2038-1 (sc)

Print information available on the last page.

iUniverse rev. date: 07/31/2021

Dedicated to:
Keith and Willy Hageman
(of St. Paul, Minnesota) and Bridget
of Villa Rica, Peru ...Dlsiluk

Acknowledgements:

Special thanks to Poet and Journalist, Apolinario Mayta Inga, for his
Journalistic support and inspiration in this project (Juan Parra del Riego's
translated poetry);
To Cesar Gamarra, television cultural host, and poet, for his ongoing support and
interest in my poetic projects, in particular this book on Juan Parra del Riego; and
the young poet, journalist Jaime Bravo for his enthusiasm, in this project...

*I believe that man will prevail. He is immortal...has an inexhaustible
voice...a spirit capable of compassion and sacrifice and endurance.
The poet's, the writer's, duty is to write about these things."*

From William Faulkner's
Nobel Prize Speech, 1950

The Virtues of a country are expressed by its poets.

Dlsiluk, 1-2009

*Note: the translations in this book are that of a Peruvian
Spanish, to American English*

The Days

By Dennis L. Siluk, Ed.D (Poet Laureate)
(Tribute to Juan Parra del Riego)

I

All year, knowing you're dead,
I've sat in two hard-pillowed chairs,
Looking out the windows, being sad
With human melancholy, trying to restart
Those days in which you lived your poetry—
(in translating, editing, and selecting your best),
Days when your youth like mine, felt the sun
Carried ambition, from earth to sky,
Ominous days, with inspiration to share;
I live them now, but feel yours in death.

II

Today, is like any day, I suppose
As you once knew, expected death,
As I do now. The sky is overcast,
(I hear the shuddering rain, the splash
As cars driving by, with purring engines)—
And in the rush, like a river off-course,
This is the moment when the air
Being most full of life and images,
Appears lifeless, no motion, now:
Land, river and sky, we merge, the
Splash is gone. And so is my sadness.
Everything is drowned out of me, but you
(so I can write this poetic tribute).
My memories emerge (with them), I've found
The days you lived, the key to your poetry;
The secret closet you hid as a poet.

III

I think of all you did, when you lived
(That is, all you wrote, and might have wrote
And done before death undid you…despair)
There was much promise in your youthful
Years--your wild reserve, the color of autumn leaves
In your Face, inspiring the wind, and woods
And the bare silence in the hummingbirds.

2

None had such promise then, not even
Cesar Vallejo, or Borges, not even Yeats,
Or Keats, GeorgeTrakl, or Pablo Neruda.
Your rhythm and rhyme, scapegrace charm,
Pattern and structure of sound, verse and meter,
Accentual-syllabic line, all gave motion
As if glazed in rain, falling hard to soft...with
Disarming grace, yes, oh yes, you were bold,
As Homer, building a wooden horse
To Deceive and then destroy Troy!
In the Age of Symbolism and Modernism.

It was, was it not, in your luckless blood?
That failure came only because all passion
Was taken away in mid-course? By Death!
You shrank to nothingness, but still you
Wrote your poetry, an hour before your death!
You lived beyond the gloomy boredom of regret.
You did not deject any love, the beat of your heart,
Was for Blanca Luz Brum, no cold fortune...
Your slow death, shaped your stare upon life
There was blood within that sightless stare,
But it made you one, made you look and wrote
Your poetry in stone, at the end, alone...

IV

Your poetry has outlived you, and that sightless stare.
Your poetry Parra, has outlive that boat you rowed—
So long ago, in Montevideo and it will
Outlive the painting that hung in your room
Where you sat by a table— the ultimate last hours
Before your death (with Blanca Luz and an *amigo*)...

I see the grief upon her youthful face, drunk
With loss, seeking some oblivious place, to hide in
Desolation, despondency, mouth open as if in horror,
Eyes staring, for the haunted hour is near, harrowing
Face, full of disgrace...for being helpless!
She holds hard onto her chair, legs half crossed,
Breathing slowly, she knows soon, what she must endure.

V

Blanca and Juan's *amigo*, stood by him the hour
Of his humiliation, yet he did not turn upon them
In the last hours of the night—they in a sad self-
Loathing, Juan, concealing nothing,
He heard Blanca cry, "I am lost. But you are worse!"

3

Perhaps the dying do not own to their dominance.
But this night, the lights were lowered,
It was the later hour,
And then the lights went out,

then the dissipation of the night passed...

Everybody worn-out, utter destitution
And the two now knew, the world deprived!

VI

Knowing, and having heard, read the bare fact
Of your death, the word lingers in my head--
Death in that haunting room,
Shut tight, from sky and cloud,
Only silent thoughts, cast from
Moment to moment, to illume later on
With those loved ones by your side
...

The hours you and I have now known,
Even though you've been dead over eighty-years,
Neither denounces my poem, tribute for you,
Nor pardons, my words, if they offend...
Like you, I have seen the moon's light, glide
Upon, and over the sea's tide, and the waves
Lost on the sandy shore, as they recede never
To succumb to them even when the dark has come;
I hope I am strong as you (when my death comes),
Although I cannot promise what I cannot give...

and now to your Surpassed fame, O'dark!
    you have turned into light!

Written 12-24-2008 (Morning); Huancayo, Peru, No: 2533

Los Días

Por Dr. Dennis L. Siluk, Ed.D (Poeta Laureado)
(Tributo a Juan Parra del Riego)

I

Todo el año, sabiendo que estás muerto,
Me he sentado en un sillón con dos cojines,
Mirando por la ventana, estando triste
Con melancolía humana, tratando de revivir
Aquellos días en que viviste tus poesías—
(traduciéndolas, editándolas y seleccionando tus mejores),
Días cuando tu juventud como la mía, sintieron el sol
Llevar ambición, desde la tierra hasta el cielo,
Días siniestros, con inspiración para compartir;
Ahora los vivo, pero siento los tuyos en la muerte.

II

Hoy, es como otro día, supongo
Como tú una vez lo supiste, muerte esperada,
Como yo lo sé ahora. El cielo está nublado,
(Escucho la estremecedora lluvia, las salpicaduras
Mientras los carros pasan, sus motores ruidosos)
Y en la prisa, como un río fuera de curso, ahora
Es el momento cuando el aire
Estando principalmente lleno de vida e imágenes,
Aparece sin vida, sin movimiento, ahora:
Tierra, río y cielo, nos fusionamos, las
Salpicaduras se han ido. Y también mi tristeza.
Todo es ahogado en mi, pero no tú
(por eso puedo escribir este tributo poético)
Mis memorias emergen (con ellos), he encontrado
Los días que tú viviste, la llave a tus poesías:
El armario secreto que escondiste como poeta.

III

Pienso en todo lo que hiciste, cuando viviste
(Es decir, todo lo que escribiste y pudiste escribir
Y hecho antes que la muerte te llevara…desesperación)
Hubo mucha promesa en tus años
Jóvenes—tu reserva entusiasta, el color de las hojas de otoño
En tu cara, inspirando al viento, y bosques
Y al silencio desnudo en los picaflores.

Ninguno tuvo tal promesa entonces, no aún
César Vallejo, o Borges, no aún Yeats,

O Kyats, George Trakl, o Pablo Neruda.
Tu ritmo y rima, encanto astuto,
Modelo y estructura del sonido, verso y medida,
Líneas silábicas acentuadas, todo daban movimiento
Como cristales en la lluvia, cayendo con fuerza y suave...con
Gracia desarmada, si, o si, tú fuiste audaz,
Como Homero, construyendo su caballo de madera
¡Para engañar y luego destruir a Troya!
En la Edad del Simbolismo y Modernismo.

Esto estaba en tu sangre desafortunada ¿cierto?
Esa falla vino sólo porque toda pasión
Estaba siendo quitada a mitad del recorrido ¡Por la muerte!
Tú te redujiste a la nada, pero aún
Escribiste tu poesía, ¡una hora antes de tu muerte!
Tú viviste más allá del sombrío aburrimiento de pesar.
Tú no afligiste a ningún amor, los latidos de tu corazón,
Fueron para Blanca Luz Brum...
Tu muerte lenta, moldeó tu mirada sobre la vida
Había sangre dentro de esa mirada ciega,
Pero esto te hizo uno, te hizo mirar y escribir
Tu poesía en piedra, al final, solo...

IV

Tu poesía te ha sobrevivido, y a esa mirada ciega.
Tu poesía, Parra, ha sobrevivido aquel bote que remaste—
Mucho tiempo atrás, en Montevideo y esta
Sobrevivirá a la pintura colgada en la pared de tu cuarto
Donde te sentaste cerca de una mesa—las últimas horas
Antes de tu muerte (con Blanca Luz y un amigo)...

Veo el dolor en su cara joven, embriagada
Con pérdida, buscando algún lugar tranquilo, para esconderse
En desolación, abatida, boquiabierta como si en horror,
Ojos mirando, porque la hora atribulada está cerca,
Cara desgarradora, llena de desgracia... ¡por ser impotente!
Ella se agarra fuerte de su silla, sus piernas medias cruzadas,
Respirando lentamente, ella sabe pronto, lo que debe de sufrir.

V

Blanca y el amigo de Juan estuvieron cerca de él la hora
De su degradación, aunque él no se volteó hacia ellos
En las últimas horas de la noche—ellos en una triste
Auto aversión, Juan, sin nada que ocultar,
Él oyó gritar a Blanca, "Estoy perdida, pero tú estás peor"

Talvez el moribundo no poseía a sus dominios,
Pero esta noche, las luces estaban bajas,
Era la última hora,
Y luego las luces se apagaron,

entonces la disipación de la noche pasó....

Todos rendidos, en completa penuria
Y los dos ahora supieron, ¡el mundo se privó!

VI

Sabiendo y habiendo oído, leído sobre la verdad desnuda
De tu muerte, la palabra perdura en mi cabeza—
Muerte en ese cuarto tormentoso,
Cerrado fuertemente, desde el cielo y nubes,
Sólo pensamientos silenciosos, echados de
Momento a momento, para iluminar más tarde
Con aquellos seres amados por tu lado
...

Las horas que tú y yo ahora conocemos,
A pesar de que tú estás muerto más de ochenta años,
Ni denuncia mi poema, un tributo para ti,
Ni perdona, mis palabras, si ellas ofenden...
Como tú, he visto la luz de la luna, deslizarse
Encima, y sobre la marea del mar, y las olas
Perdidas en las orillas arenosas, mientras ellas se retiran
Para nunca sucumbir a ellos aun cuando la oscuridad ha llegado;
Espero que yo sea fuerte como tú (cuando mi muerte llegue),
Aunque no puedo prometer lo que no puedo dar...

Y ahora a tu fama superada, ¡oh oscuridad!
    ¡Tú te has transformado en luz!

Escrito el 24-Dic.-2008 en la mañana, en Huancayo, Perú. Nro. 2533

Recent Awards given to the author:
Dennis L. Siluk:

Awarded the Prize Excellence: The Poet & Writer of 2006 by Corporacion de Prensa Autonoma (of the Mantaro Valley of Peru)

Awarded the National Prize of Peru by Antena Regional: The best of 2006 for promoting culture.

Poet Laureate of San Jeronimo de Tunan, Peru (2005); and the Mantaro Valley (8-2007) (Awarded the (Gold) Grand Cross of the City (2006))

Lic. Dennis L. Siluk, awarded a medal of merit, and diploma from the Journalists Professional Association of Peru, in August of 2007, for his international attainment.

On November 26, 2007, Lic. Dennis L. Siluk was nominated, Poet Laureate of Cerro de Pasco and received recognition as an Illustrious Visitor of the Cities of Cerro de Pasco, and Huayllay, Peru.

"Union Mathematic School" (Huancayo, Peru), Honor to the Merit to: Lic. Dennis Lee Siluk Ed.D. (Awarded) Poet and Writer Excellence of 2007, for contributing to the culture and regional identity, Huancayo. December 1, 2007, Signed: Pedro Guillen, Director.

The Sociologists Professional Association of Peru, Central Region, granted to Dr. Dennis Lee Siluk, Writer Laureate for his professional contribution in the social interaction of the towns and rescue of their identity. Huancayo December 6, 2007 —Lic. Juan Condori –Senior Member of the Sociologists Professional Association.

The Association of Broadcasters of the Central Region of Peru, nominated Dr. Dennis Lee Siluk Honorary Member for his works done on the Central Region of Peru; in addition, the Mayor of Huancayo, Freddy Arana Velarde, gave Dr. Siluk, 'Reconocimiento de Honor,' and 'Illustrious Personage...' status (December, 2007).

The Peruvian North American Cultural Institute granted to Dr. Siluk a "Diploma of Honor" for his important contribution to the propagation of the cultural Andean values. Huancayo – Perú, December 28, 2007. Signed: Director of Culture: Diana V. Casas R. and President of the Directive Board: Alfonso Velit Nunez.

Diploma of Recognition, awarded to Dennis Siluk, Poet Laureate, by the Editor Jose Arrieta, of the magazine, "Destacados," Sept, 2008, for "Heroic Enterprising and contribution in development of the economic, social educational and cultural Region of Junin, Peru (in, 2007)".

Awarded "Honorary Member" of the Journalists Professional Association of Peru (The Journalists Professional Association of Peru granted Dr. Dennis Lee Siluk

Honorary Membership and authorizes him to practice the profession in the Peruvian territory. Lima, October 1st, 2008)

Radio Acknowledgement: many of Mr. Siluk's poems were read on live radio, on: "Poetry Moment," on FM 89.5, University Radio, on Tuesdays and Thursdays (12:20 PM), in the months of October and November 2007, in Huancayo, Peru. Hosted by Eduardo Cardenas, and read in Spanish by Rosa Peñaloza de Siluk, and in English by Dennis L. Siluk.

The Council (ruling body) of the Continental University, of Huancayo, Peru, congratulates and recognizes Dr. Dennis Lee Siluk for his abundant intellectual contribution (with his writings), permitting the Mantaro Valley's attributes to be known worldwide. November, 27, 2008 (Resolution No. 309-2008 CU/UCCI-2008, signed by Dr. Esau Tiberio Caro Meza, Rector, and Dr. Armando Prieto Hormaza, General Secretary.

Acknowledgment from the National Institute of Culture of District of Villa Rica, Oxapampa, Pasco, Peru, given to Dennis Lee Siluk, for his participation in the Literature *"Nuestras Voces,"* in conjunction with the 64th Anniversary of the District, 29 November of 2008.

Diploma given to Dr. Dennis Lee Siluk, as Writer and Talent of the Poetry of the year 2007, by Antena Regional (*Edición de Premiación Anual de Costa, Sierra y Selva*).

Letters and Acknowledgements to
The Author Dennis L. Siluk, Ed.D.

Some Letters sent to the author by the well-known:

President Ronald Reagan, March, 1985, letter sent on behalf of the book, "The Safe Child/The Unsafe child" as indicated in Roseville Focus," Minnesota (USA) newspaper, article: "Author Helps Kids be safe," March 18, 1985.

President Jimmy Carter, on behalf of one of Mr. Siluk's books, 2003

President George W. Bush (three letters), one in particular, in July, 2001, thanking the author for his support, notes on the nation and one of the author's books.

Also Mr. Siluk has received letters between 2002, and 2007, from Arial Sharon (Prime Minister of Israel: Ref: book sent him, ("Islam, In Search of Satan's Rib"); the Dalai Lama; and from the office of the Republic of Cuba, State Council, signed by Fidel Castro, Ex President of Cuba.

Also a letter from Senior Senator Keiko Fujimori of Peru (about the conversation they had in person concerning the poetic cultural book, "The Road to Unishcoto," in which she appears); and the prominent historian Dr. Maria Rostworowski in an historical meeting between the two, talking about the customs and foods of the Mantaro Valley of Peru.

Mr. Siluk received two favorable letters, from the Pulitzer Prize Entry Committee, acknowledging and praising his works, one in 1982 for the poetic tale "The Tale of Willie the Humpback Whale," and the other in 1985, concerns the book: "The Safe Child and the Unsafe Child (put into the National Library at Washington D.C."

◆◆

Some acknowledgements to the Author

Dennis has been on Television some thirty-times, on Radio, over sixty, in the newspapers (over 40-times) from Minnesota, North Dakota (the Midwest in General) to include C.S.P., World News; he has received two columnist awards in the United States, and an Honorary award, as National Journalist of Peru (along with many awards from professional associations of Peru, such as, the Professional Association of Sociologists of the Central Region of Peru, who has acclaimed his cultural works; and the acclaimed, school of Huancayo, Colegio Matematico Union "Honor al Merito", known for its outstanding students worldwide (in which they now hold the gold medal).

The Selected Poetry, Life and Times of: Juan Parra del Riego

Index of Poems, Commentaries and Other Works

12

Additional poems by:
Juan Parra del Riego

(Selected poems extracted in Spanish from the book: "MAÑANA CON EL ALBA Obra Poética Completa", 1994 translated by: Dennis L. Siluk, Ed.D, and Rosa Peñaloza de Siluk

The Vidalita
Her Laugh
The Windmills
The Park
Far

✝

Two Accompanying Poems: Christmas and Kisses

Magic Christmas Eve

"Kisses"
(A poem with commentary notes)

♦

Two Pigeons Kissing
A poem by Dlsiluk as a tribute to Juan Parra del Riego's poem, 'Kisses'

Overview of:
The Life and Times of Blanca Luz Brum
(Wife of Juan Parra del Riego)
See Article in Back of Book

Other books by the Author

The Selected Translated Poetry, of:

Juan Parra del Riego

Δ

The Translated Poetry of Juan Parra del Riego

Chosen and Translated

By

Dennis L. Siluk and Rosa Peñaloza de Siluk

**With Introduction and Commentaries
(Biography); Editing by Dennis L. Siluk**

First Time Ever Translated into English

An Ode To:

Juan Parra del Riego

By Dennis L. Siluk

Juan, king of poets of Peru, farthest bound
and the poet of Huancayo—so crowned.
Behold, the fires of your words are now drawn.
Bring forth your poems, we beckon at dawn.
By some new echoes in the cosmic tone—
on Earth, you have risen to heights unknown.

Dedícate to Juan Parra del Riego
No: 1918 7-25-07 (JPR born in Huancayo, Peru)

Una Oda para:

Juan Parra del Riego

Por Dennis L. Siluk

Juan, rey de los poetas de Perú, fuera de límites
y el poeta de Huancayo—tan coronado.
Mira, los fuegos de tus palabras son ahora dibujados.
Produce tus poemas, nosotros llamamos al amanecer.
Con algunos ecos nuevos en el tono cósmico—
en la tierra, tú te has elevado a alturas desconocidas.

Dedicado a Juan Parra del Riego, quien nació en Huancayo, Perú.
1918 25-Julio-2007

15

Portrait of Juan Parra, by Dennis L. Siluk (2007)

By Dennis L. Siluk

Born, 1894, died 1925; from Huancayo, Peru (Juan Parra del Riego)

JUAN PARRA DEL RIEGO'S BIOGRAPHY

Juan Parra del Riego was born on December 20, 1894 in the city of Huancayo, Peru; his parents were Domingo Parra Aubilá and Mercedes Rodríguez Gonzáles del Riego. Juan passed his childhood in Arequipa, studied at the College of the "American Independence," then with his family he moved to Cuzco (Peru), where he took up studies at the National College of Sciences and Art in the city.

At this time, in the city of Cuzco at the college the poet to be, was awaken to his calling, and quickly demonstrated his skill not only in poetry but in football, which he would write about competently in future years.

Juan then moved to Lima with his family, where he lived his vocation: poetry, by pursuing the art and craft of verse writing; and at the early age of nineteen-years old was awarded his first Gold Medal at the First Floral Games organized by the District Municipality of Surco with his poem called, "Canto to Barranco."

His poetry was published in many of Peru's newspapers, and while visiting Trujillo, he became friends with Cesar Vallejo.

In 1916 at only 22- years of age, he made a trip in search of the "American and Universal Citizenship," visiting Chile where he met Gabriela Mistral, then he visited Argentina and Uruguay, where he was nourished with the era's literary movements.

During this time he embarked on a trip to Europe, traveling across Holland, Spain and France, into Paris, which dazzled him.

During most of these years, and travels his health remained marginal to manageable to intense.

In 1925 he met the lady poet Blanca Luz Brum with whom he married and had a son with, named Eduardo (see more on this and photo, at the end of the book).

Juan's health became very fragile but had a transmittable desire for living as one can see by reading many of his poems. In a short period of time his lungs gave out, damaged beyond repair, he was then taken to the Military Hospital in Montevideo, where on November 21, 1925 he died. The president of the Republic of the Uruguay, Jose Serrato, decreed a national holiday and set the Uruguayan flag at half mast. He was buried in the Cemetery of *Buceo.*

Note: information extracted from literature by Apolinario Mayta Inga, and Klim Kafra, all parts reedited by Dennis L. Siluk, and revised; translated from the Spanish to English and back into the Spanish by Rosa de Peñaloza de Siluk; as it has been prepared for a forthcoming book. (Note: August, 2007)

BIOGRAFÍA DE JUAN PARRA DEL RIEGO

Juan Parra del Riego nació el 20 de diciembre de 1894 en la ciudad de Huancayo, Perú; sus padres fueron don Domingo Parra Aubilá y doña Mercedes Rodríguez Gonzáles del Riego. Juan pasó su niñez en Arequipa, estudió en el Colegio "Independencia Americana", luego con toda su familia se trasladó a Cuzco (Perú), donde estudió en el Colegio Nacional de Ciencias y Arte en esa ciudad.

En este tiempo, en la ciudad de Cuzco y en ese colegio el que iba a ser un poeta, fue despertando a ese llamado, y rápidamente demostraba su habilidad no sólo en la poesía sino en el fútbol, del que él escribiría competentemente en años futuros.

Juan se trasladó a Lima con su familia, donde vivió su vocación: la poesía, perseverando en el arte y oficio de los versos escritos; y a la temprana edad de diecinueve años fue premiado con su primera Medalla de Oro en los Primeros Juegos Florales organizado por el Concejo Distrital de Surco con su poema llamado, "Canto a Barranco".

Sus poesías fueron publicadas en muchos periódicos de Perú, y mientras visitaba Trujillo entabló amistad con César Vallejo.

En 1916 con tan sólo veintidós años de edad, hizo un viaje en busca de la "Ciudadanía Americana y Universal" visitando Chile donde conoció a Gabriela Mistral, luego visitó Argentina y Uruguay, donde fue nutrido con el movimiento literario de esa época.

Durante este tiempo él se embarcó en un viaje a Europa, viajando a través de Holanda, España y Francia, hacia París, ciudad que lo deslumbró.

Durante la mayor parte de estos años y viajes, su salud permanecía marginal e iba deteriorándose.

En 1925 Juan conoció a la poetisa Blanca Luz Brum con quien contrajo matrimonio y tuvieron un hijo al que llamó

Eduardo (ver más información y fotos al final del libro).

La salud de Juan se volvió muy frágil pero él tenía un deseo contagioso por vivir como uno puede ver leyendo sus muchos poemas. En corto tiempo sus pulmones se deterioraron, dañados al punto de no tener cura; él fue llevado al Hospital Militar en Montevideo, donde el 21 de noviembre de 1925 murió. El Presidente de la República de Uruguay, José Serrato, decretó duelo nacional y ordenó izar la bandera uruguaya a media asta. Fue enterrado en el Cementerio de Buceo.

Nota: información extraída de la literatura de Apolinario Mayta Inga y Klim Kafra, todo reeditado y revisado por Dennis L. Siluk; traducido del español al inglés y del inglés al español por Rosa Peñaloza de Siluk; ya que este ha sido preparado para un próximo libro.

A Compilation of: thoughts, and

notes on:
Juan Parra del Riego (and his brother Carlos)
By Dennis L. Siluk

1—It should be noted, Cesar Vallejo was forty-six years old when he died, and Juan Parra del Riego was 31; Vallejo born 1892, died 1938, and Riego born 1894, died 1925, both were friends. Two years apart in age. Both Great poets, but for my money I would take Juan Parra before Vallejo; he is the greatest modern poet in Uruguay, and not quite that well known in Peru, although Huancayo, where he was born, he is clearly a name recognized; unfortunately, his books are not sold in any bookstores there, up to this writing anyhow.

2—To my knowledge one has yet to write a full biography of Parra del Riego in English, or translate his poetry, in quantity, and quality, the contents in this book (and on a site I created for him on the internet in English and Spanish) is the closest thing to one; with some poems.

3—We know like Vallejo, Juan went to Paris, and had to borrow money to get back home, thus, he ended up poor, as most poets do, a few exceptions who have received inheritances to help them make it through life.

4—A reader may ask, "Just what can we learn from this Peruvian poet?" This would in itself give justification for publishing, editing, and translating his poetry and background. I mean it was no easy task to do. First of all, scarcely does anyone know the existence of this great poet in North America, Asia, or Europe; as they didn't know about Vallejo, until Robert Bly (North American Poet) translated his works in back in 1962. I have tried to bring this poet stamina and imagination to bear

21

on the hunger and pain he faced, while writing his poetry, for he was dying during the process, thus we see a different kind of reality here. We see his inner world, almost his soul within his poetry; this is why I think he is an import poet to read, study, and simply enjoy.

5—Juan Parra del Riego, is an authentic poet with deep feeling. He does not hide the difficult parts of his life, which are often full of despair, and dim lights, he describes it with love and paces rapidly to and fro, the master of Polirritmo in the time of Modernism in poetry (1914 to 1965).There is tenderness, rowdiness, hunger, restlessness, and compassion for life in his poetry).

6—Carlos Parra del Riego, one of Juan Parra del Riego's brothers, was also a poet in his own right, and like his older brother Juan, died also of tuberculosis. He got his illness in Argentina, and in 1936, came back to Huancayo, Peru for a cure. He lived in Huancayo for another three years and died (also lived part time in Jauja). He was hospitalized most of the time. His writings, "Why I killed the child," and "Romantic Serenade," both done in prose style poetry.

The Works of Juan Parra del Riego

Some of his works were dispersed in magazines and newspapers, and can be enumerated this way (and books):

- "The Truth of the Lie" (1915 - Lima)

- "Anthem of the Sky and of the Railroads" (1925 - Montevideo)

- "Blanca Luz" (1925 - Montevideo)

- "Three Unpublished Polirritmos" (1937 - Montevideo)

- "Poem" (1943 - Montevideo)

- "Poems" (1972-Huancayo)

- "Poems and Polirritmos" (1988 - Lima)

- PROSA (1943, Uruguay)

Juan Parra del Riego's Poetry

Poem One

English Version

THE WINDS OF PERU

There is nothing in this world, nor the sun, or in war
as to the wild winds of this land!

Neither the bladelike profile of the Sierras,
nor the streaks of lightening that vibrate, nor the thunder that terrifies,
nor the same flash of lightening that opens and closes
and the sea that grips the beaches... grips...

There is nothing in this world, nor the sun, or in war
as to the wild winds of this land!

Brisk winds that wave handkerchiefs
of dust in the escape of the big flights,
but softer than the velvets
when they crash of vague desires
seems that then they come down from the skies
with the madness of a thousand exhortations.
They would leave dancing without stepping on the ground
the lighthearted dance of the veils.
I recall the tropical blasts
because of a hundred bronze trumpets in choir
I owe to them this gesture, which I never implore,
nor do I tremble, neither do I cry ...
I recall the tropical blasts
when in the plains where the bull bellows
and the horse makes happy its resonant sounds
they twist into golden spinning tops.

There is nothing in this world, nor the sun, or in war
as to the wild winds of this land!

Casuhiras of the forest, jumping felines

that scratch and climb the thin trees
and playing to the game of the vortex
 - Oh, blue drunkenness of divine pleasures! -
they sound in the branches, sing in the pines
and roll behind the peasants
who in the evenings return for those ways
where the road of weary oxen
looks as if to cry, likened to the mills.
Vicious proprietors at first light
half-open closed doors, in the countryside
likened to a nervous driving force,
I learned by you my rough tunes
and to go for the world as the waterfalls:
jumping, impulses, winged roads
and I do not know what anxiety on sacred summits
but it makes me become an unfolded sail
for the deepest ignored routes.
Ocean cyclones that initiate a journey
that never stops on the wild seas.
And jeer to the lash of a mad carriage
which is the runaway vision of the landscape.
Break the statues that carve the surge
they attack the vessels upon the boarding.
And as in *Esquilo* they say a language
that is more the tragedy of a wild soul.

There is nothing in this world, nor the sun, or in war
as to the wild winds of this land!

In the sensitive rural mornings
the tempest of the dramatic *Mascaichas*
—smell of the water virgins, to the jungles and cornfields!—
Oh, dizzy cheerful satyrs
that to the peasants of fruit-bearing bosoms
throw mad the slight percales
as if they wanted, drunks and sensual
to take them rapidly up to the wheat fields…
I still have not forgotten that I come from those
cities with manly summits of epics
under the golden vineyards that exist in the stars.
If I feel in my blood the fluttering signs
of those wild and sweet maidens
whom to the Spanish— were dances and sparks—
for seeing Atahualpa die, together with them
were saying soft as the stars

such sad things…and so beautiful things…
Winds, winds, winds of my land, lions
that the dust curls with its cottons,
let's go frantic for the towns
of this old America with its traditions
that makes of its people servants and clowns.
Devastatingly, and sadly, let us sing songs
that shake like pistons to the hearts,
refreshes the souls and lifts the passions
in the red lances of other rebellions.

There is nothing in this world, nor the sun, or in war
as to the wild winds of this land!

Spanish Version

LOS VIENTOS DEL PERÚ

¡No hay nada en el mundo, ni el sol, ni la guerra
como los salvajes vientos de esta tierra!

Ni el acuchillado perfil de la sierra,
ni el rayo que vibra, ni el trueno que aterra,
ni el mismo relámpago que abre y se cierra
y el mar que en las playas se aferra…se aferra…

¡No hay nada en el mundo, ni el sol, ni la guerra
como los salvajes vientos de esta tierra¡

Aires ululantes que agitan pañuelos
de polvo en la fuga de los grandes vuelos,
pero que más suaves que los terciopelos
cuando se entrechocan de vagos anhelos
parece que entonces bajó de los cielos
y en una locura de mil ritornelos
se fueran bailando sin pisar los suelos
la vertiginosa danza de los velos.

Tropicales ráfagas que yo rememoro
porque a sus cien rubias trompetas en coro
les debo este gesto con que nunca imploro,
con que nunca tiemblo, con que nunca lloro…

26

Tropicales ráfagas que yo rememoro
cuando en las llanuras donde muge el toro
y el caballo alegra su clarín sonoro
se iban dando vueltas como trompos de oro.

¡No hay nada en el mundo, ni el sol, ni la guerra
como los salvajes vientos de esta tierra!

Casuhiras del monte, saltantes felinos
que arañan y trepan los árboles finos
y jugando al juego de los remolinos
-¡Oh, azul borrachera de goces divinos!-
suenan en las ramas, cantan en los pinos
y se van rodando tras los campesinos
que en las tardes vuelven por esos caminos
donde la carretera de bueyes cansinos
parece que llora como los molinos.

Pamperos violentos que en las madrugadas
del campo entreabrían las puertas cerradas
como a una nerviosa lucha de estocadas,
yo aprendí en vosotros mis rudas tonadas
y el ir por el mundo como las cascadas:
a saltos, impulsos, carreteras aladas
y no sé que angustia de cumbres sagradas
que me hace ser todo velas desplegadas
para las más hondas rutas ignoradas.

Ciclones marinos que inician un viaje
Que nunca se para sobre el mar salvaje.

Y pifian la fusta de un loco carruaje
que es la desbocada visión del paisaje.

Rompen las estatuas que esculpe el oleaje,
atacan los buques como al abordaje.

Y como en Esquilo dicen un lenguaje
que es más la tragedia de un alma salvaje.

¡No hay nada en el mundo, ni el sol, ni la guerra
como los ciclones del mar de esta tierra!

Mascaichas dramáticos de los temporales

en las sensitivas mañanas rurales
-¡olor a aguas vírgenes, a las selvas y maizales!-

¡Oh, vertiginosos sátiros joviales
que a las campesinas de senos frutales
tirábanles locos los leves percales
como si quisieran, ebrios y sensuales
llevarles rápido hasta los trigales…

Yo aún no me he olvidado que vengo de aquellas
ciudades con cumbre viril de epopeyas
bajo el parral de oro que hay en las estrellas.

¡Si aun siento en mi sangre palpitar las huellas
de aquellas salvajes y dulces doncellas
que a los españoles –danzas y centellas-
por ver a Atahualpa morir junto a ellas
les decían suaves como las estrellas
qué cosas tan tristes…qué cosas tan bellas…
Vientos, vientos, vientos de mi tierra, leones
que el polvo enmelena con sus algodones,
vámonos frenéticos por las poblaciones
de esta vieja América con sus tradiciones
que hacen de las gentes siervos y bufones.

Y arrollantes, trágicos, rompamos canciones
Que agiten como émbolos a los corazones,
refresquen las almas y alcen las pasiones
en las rojas lanzas de otras rebeliones.

¡No hay nada en el mundo, ni el sol, ni la guerra
como los salvajes vientos de esta tierra.!

Poem Two

CANTO TO BARRANCO
(The Sea)

Sea by Barranco, the meditating sea,
sad sea, sea without sails, asleep sea,
my pain is bitter and is deep
because on seeing you, your sorrow I have taken.
If you have your shipwrecked persons, oh Sea!
that denies the appearance of your calmness
I also like you ... know how to disguise
the shipwrecked illusions of my soul.
Like this sun that sinks sadly, sadly,
in your confines of gold and red dressings
thus they are sinking slow, slow,
when before your broad face I dream and ponder,
in your blue secret ... my thoughts
like endless drunken birds.

Spanish Version

CANTO A BARRANCO
(El Mar)

Mar de Barranco, mar meditabundo,
mar triste, mar sin velas, mar dormido,
mi dolor es amargo y es profundo
porque al verte tu pena he cogido.
Si tú tienes tus náufragos ¡oh mar!
que niega la apariencia de tu calma
yo también como tú sé enmascarar
las ilusiones náufragas de mi alma.
Como ese sol que se hunde triste, triste,
en tu confín que de oro y grana viste,
así se van hundiendo lentos, lentos,
cuando ante tu ancha faz sueño y medito,
en tu secreto azul mis pensamientos
como pájaros ebrios de infinito.

Poem three

DYNAMIC *POLIRRITMO* OF THE MOTORCYCLE

Slanted in the wind the warm keel of the definite profile
and free the spirit to the day like a kite
every evening I launch into the tumult of the avenues
on a vibrating iron horse
my motorcycle!
Hum the pedals; quivers the tire
and in the feverish fiery of the engine
I feel that there is something
that is like my burning throat
with my explosive secret interior.
And I run ... run ... run ...
across the city, with the thrust of my noise
sight a boulevard and trend avenues...
dislocate a corner
and wrap in the wheels
the dizzy palpitating stretch of the streets ....
The shooting reflections of the bulbs, breaks the
illumination....
And I launch to a blast, and race to the sea
And again I escape for the boulevards,
rapid serpents of cars and hats,
women and bars
and lights and workers
who pass and hit and escape and return again ....
And I run ... run ... run ...
until high and quite pale
of danger and sky and dizziness in my bold speed
already my soul is not my soul:
it is a piston with music
a wild warm top,
all the dream of the life that in my chest I inflame and weep
the happy race of gold
of the naked and free light that will never leave us.
Ah, run madly convinced
in reaching as the birds up to the blue limit,
listening, inclined,
to the hearing,

the engine,
as if it was the nervous heart of a friend
which burns in a stubborn secret of love!
The eyes rob the life out of themselves unto pieces!
Lights, men, trees, a star...the sea,
and I only feel
a mad desire to be like the wind
that seems as if it wants to pass.
Soft curve,
pathetic "X"... attack.
Sudden dry clutch ... sudden turn ... explosion!
Was it the death? Was it the life?
The engine suffers and trembles
and again the wind soaks me with its wine and heart.
Comrades! Comrades!
Give me a T-shirt
of violent green and golden colors that glitter
to sink and crack with my
motorcycle
within the shuddering fields in this evening of colors.
In the galloping horse
his flushed blood sounds
to open every evening of his life
to a romantic moment of departure.
To depart ... to arrive ... to arrive ... to depart...
To run ...
to fly ...
to die ...
to dream ...
To depart ...to depart ...to depart ...

Spanish Version

POLIRRITMO DINAMICO DE LA MOTOCICLETA

Sesgada en el viento la cálida quilla del perfil tajante
y suelto el espíritu al día como una cometa
yo todas las tardes me lanzo al tumulto de las avenidas
sobre un trepidante caballo de hierro
¡mi motocicleta!
Zumban los pedales, palpita la llanta
y en la traquearteria febril del motor
yo siento que hay algo

que es como mi ardiente garganta
con mi explosionante secreto interior.
Y corro...corro...corro...
Estocada de mi ruido que atraviesa la ciudad
y ensarto avenidas...suspiro una rambla...disloco una
esquina
y envuelvo en las ruedas
la vertiginosa cinta palpitante de las alamedas...
La fusilería de los focos rompe la iluminación...
Y me lanzo a un tiro de carrera al mar
Y otra vez me escapo por los bulevares,
rápidas serpientes de autos y sombreros,
mujeres y bares
y luces y obreros
que pasan y chocan y fugan y vuelven de nuevo a pasar...
Y corro...corro...corro...
hasta que ebrio y todo pálido
de peligro y cielo y vértigo en mi audaz velocidad
ya mi alma no es mi alma:
es un émbolo con música
un salvaje trompo cálido,
todo el sueño de la vida que en mi pecho incendio y lloro
la feliz carrera de oro
de la luz desnuda y libre que jamás nos dejará.
¡Ah, correr locamente convencido
de alcanzar como los pájaros hasta el confín azul,
escuchando, inclinado,
al oído,
el motor,
cual si fuera el nervioso corazón de un amigo
que se quema en un terco secreto de amor!
¡Los ojos se roban la vida a pedazos!
Luces, hombres, árboles, una estrella...el mar,
y ya solo siento
un deseo loco de ser como el viento
que sólo parece que quiere pasar.
Curva suave,
X patética...embestida.
Repentino embrague seco...vuelta súbita...explosión!
¿Fue la muerte? ¿Fue la vida?
el motor sufre y trepida
y otra vez me empapa el viento con su vino el corazón.
¡Camaradas! ¡Camaradas!
denme una camiseta
de violentas pintas verdes y oros como resplandores

para hundirme a puñaladas
de motocicleta
por el campo estremecido de esta tarde de colores.
En el fulminante
caballo que suena su sangre encendida
para abrir todas las tardes de la vida
a un romántico momento de partida.
Partir...llegar...llegar...partir...
Correr...
volar...
morir...
soñar...
partir...partir...partir...

Poem Four

English Version

Night Nro. 8

Hurting in the moon, the road fades away
I am going to feel more today your soul, there;
Hurting in the moon that looks and waits for me
and gives its lonely carrier pigeon
memories that belong to you.
I look at the mysterious loneliness in the sky
and nothing is deeper than your love,
a dancer of bitterness, a tap dancer on ice.
Oh! Syrian, you are the sweet violinist of the sky!
Here, makes me understand you better.
For you are the light that trembles there:
I go alone. I go tired. I go blind. I go lost.
And this night of the moon, which has soundless music
it is as if your soul is put deep into a nest
and my weeping goes without end.
With my black hat awash in the moon
I tell you of my suffering.
I shall ask death for more dread to unite us…
I shall ask life for pleasant fortune
with kisses of madness and trembling.
I will tell you the history of a wandering man
that one day he launched into a bitter world.
He was the happy young wayfarer when he left
Later, bent and sad, and more out of breath
his bleeding heart, returned.
He neither became a dreamer nor a learned humorist
of those who only wish to deceive.
In life he saw the abyss was oblivion
and his great secret was to be always himself
and with a warm soul waiting....
And he saw that love was the obvious path
and for that, it was essential to survive;
—oh, much-loved, the sweetest, who encourages—
I that have departed in your soul have come to face you
yet I already realize why I have to live.
Before the moon, I know why I tremble as I poet
the time being of Musset and Jorge Sand;

in my restless city, I sometimes more than pace
I look for intimate dark quant plazas
where other warm things are.
and why my soul vibrates when I look upon a few flowers
and in the faint and blue late afternoon
words of color hum in my head.
And by the jeweler's shop, wet with brilliancies
I remain frail, as a woman.
And why, I am slower in my steps and ways
and in all, my soul knots and twists with emotion;
and there under the pines, are night guitars
in this hour comes the big sea twilights
I have a mysterious restlessness.

Spanish Version

Nocturno Nro. 8

Dolorida en la luna se va la carretera.
Me voy a sentir más hoy tu alma allí;
dolorido en la luna que me mira y espera
y da su solitaria paloma mensajera
que va como acordándose de ti.
Miro las soledades misteriosas del cielo
y nada es más profundo que tu amor,
bailarín de amargura, zapateador de hielo,
tú eres, ¡oh! Sirio, dulce violinista del cielo!
lo que me ha comprendido aquí mejor.
Pero tú eres la luz que tiembla allá:
Voy solo. Voy cansado. Voy ciego. Voy perdido.
Y esta noche de luna, que es música sin ruido
me va poniendo tu alma como en un hondo nido
sobre mi sollozante eternidad.
Con mi sombrero negro empapado en la luna
yo te contaré todo mi dolor...
Le pediré a la muerte más pavor que nos una...
le pediré a la vida más caliente fortuna
de besos, de locura y de temblor.
Yo te contaré toda mi historia de hombre errante
que un día al mundo amargo se lanzó.
Era al partir alegre el joven caminante,
más tarde, curvo y triste, pero más anhelante

su corazón, sangriento, regresó.
Y no se hizo filósofo ni aprendió el humorismo
de los que sólo quieren engañar.
Vio que en la vida sólo el olvido es el abismo
y que su gran secreto es ser siempre uno mismo
y con el alma cálida, esperar...
Y vio que el amor era la única ruta clara
y que por eso sólo hay que existir;
-¡oh, amada la más dulce, la que aclara y ampara!-
yo que he partido en tu alma y he llegado en tu cara
ya sé para qué tengo que vivir.
Sé por qué ante la luna tiemblo como un poeta
del tiempo de Musset y Jorge Sand;
y a veces más que el ritmo de mi ciudad inquieta
busco las sombras íntimas de alguna plazoleta
donde otras cosas íntimas están.
Y por qué mi alma vibra cuando miro unas flores
y en el fino y azul atardecer
en mi cabeza zumban palabras de colores,
y ante las joyerías, mojado de fulgores,
me quedo fino como una mujer.
Y porqué hago mi paso más lento en los caminos
y en todo enreda mi alma su emoción;
y bajo las guitarras nocturnas de los pinos
en la hora de los grandes crepúsculos marinos
tengo una misteriosa agitación.

Canto to the Carnival

Laughing has a wonderful freedom,
the city's carnival has a wheel of colors.
In the squares, on the towers, windows and corners,
the moon is jumping like a little girl
as the ribbons are hung around telephones
for this livid universal party.

Swings of laugher! Trees of love!
With their hearts, boyfriends warm the night.
One has already run for a dress-coat, pale he goes!
Crimson dreams
she's thinking of something sly and fantastic
that only this night might bring...

In the jingle-bells there are small elves
that say: do not doubt! Let's go to dream!
Let's go to dance!
Let's go to sing!
The night opens silk windows
and if you do not come, forever you shall remain
in the bleak pearl of waiting.
Let's go to sing!
Let's go to dance!

And on the Avenue
that burns the fruits hanging from the lighting
now the moving platforms (*floats*), lift their hallucinations
heads with masks—the great fantasy.
The sidewalk lights are happy with illumination, like a dream
port.
The houses yell, kiss and hug each other
as clouds of music and paper-ribbons
and the mad music, and painted signs
move on dreamily with its happy blaze.

Comic acrobatics...exceptional ventriloquism
from a shotgun muzzle
the black tear on a white faced clown,

under Cleopatra, a choir of trumpets
greeting to the stars and to love!
Kettledrums! Piccolos!

Insolence outrage... bizarre kites
The open air gardens are fresh and flat.
Madness, happiness, paleness, and love!
Passes the slow car of concubines,
the white group with green humor
passes the group of Ten Franciscas
and the marvelous car of the Emperor!
Queens and clowns,
- a red colored cane, flies in the air-
the comedians tangle by the moon with their steps,
drums of the east have enchanting strokes
and jumps, and reflections, nights and fruits.

Here come the blacks of sensual dance
with legs of puppets and laughs of the moon
they fall asleep on the tropical bass-drum;
these fantastic and imaginative blacks
they dramatize with vague and full of life
gestures and greetings of monkey's and goats
laughing to the spinal marrow.

A car brings a sudden *float* of angels
and then another, with *'Walkiria'* swift hairs of paper
one after another moves away throwing delightfully
jingle-bells of a crazy harlequin.
The astronomic group of the Chinese passes
-how cheerless, onward, goes the pale and sweet mandarin!
The rider cuts me
a paper-ribbon with a blue elf!
(be careful with this girl, she is like a toy
defending her wings of tulle)
and the *floats*, rise with the night, in golden arms.

Large and tropical music for the popular streets.
Behind the cloudy sorrow, of purple teeth,
this is my pirouette, my nose, my walk!
And I look at this house:
laughs from the balcony, with beards, ribbons and veils,
sounds by a window...a mask passes...
and I vision, she is with them and others
dancing to this tearful music and violoncellos ...

Silver and blue bicycles with stars run their way
towards the boulevards
jump, and rise with mocking faces,
and I am mad now, for never am I able to reach
the fantastic mouth of this thin mask,
that throughout the whole night makes me flutter.
But at this corner
four dominos have remained still,
and I am afraid at that corner
of the dominos standing up and still.
Let's go Ana!
Give me your arm Margarita!
There is a dance in this house called the bell
of a never-ending madness!
Grab me, Josefina!
I bring love to the circus with my red beard.
I know what it did not tell you, the crazy ribbon
that is in your pony-tail, it was falling asleep as if it was a
flower.
But the float passes…
Passes!
A springboard for the lively acrobat at heart!
Ditches with water, ribbons, clowns and women.
Full of wine and happiness, and their mouths of delusion
The float passes…
Passes…passes..!
Now the streets are empty and…on the ground there is a lost
mask
this last clown gets into a house where
a burning light is by a little window!

And again the *floats* go on their way
the roar of the shouting is like the sleigh-bells!
The Bears! The Fairies…the queen…the bandit…
All are tales that come out into the street
staggeringly free of their houses of paper…!
The *Volanta* of *Colombina* has arrived
—I throw this flower to the blond laughing—
The *Volanta* of *Colombina* has left
and now a serenade of paper-ribbons
go calling her in the street with their flutes of color!

Lost, ancient, gray, and sweet-smelling
pieces of music give me a shiver,
—there is a dance on those distant balconies—

and I know that she is, whose gloves these belong to
that behind her back is crystal,
a suspension of the moon
and on her black vest, a flower opens.
Passes the float with its river
which is going to get lost to the moon, with its triumphal
uproar.

And in the city, it became like a great empty theater
I feel that my heart
is walking as a lonely and ghostly cat.
The floats go away! The noise goes away
but I hang onto the magic, to your lights, and loves,
the Carnival!
An undertaking of immense health, like watering of the
flowers
that leave our heads like colorful tops
spinning, spinning, spinning,
in your hand of crystal.

Spanish Version

Canto al Carnaval

Libertad maravillosa de la risa,
la ciudad corre en las ruedas de colores, ¡Carnaval!
Ya en las plazas y torres, ventanas y esquinas,
saltando como una niñita la luna
cuelga los teléfonos de las serpentinas
para tu furiosa fiesta universal.

¡Columpios de risas! ¡Árboles de amores!
Los novios calientan la noche con su corazón.
Ya aquel ha corrido por un frac... ¡va pálido!
Rosada de sueños
ella piensa en algo furtivo y fantástico
que sólo esta noche podría pasar...

En los cascabeles hay duendes pequeños
que dicen: ¡no dudes! ¡vamos a soñar!
¡Vamos a bailar!
¡Vamos a cantar!
La noche abre dulces ventanas de seda

y si tú no vienes por siempre te quedas
en la desolada perla de esperar.
¡Vamos a cantar!
¡Vamos a bailar!
Y por la Avenida
que quema las frutas de la iluminación
ya el Corso va alzando con su delirante
cabeza de máscaras la gran ilusión.
Veredas con luces felices de puertos soñados.
Las casas se besan, se gritan, se abrazan
a nubes de música y de serpentinas,
y la opera loca de gritos pintados
avanza soñando su incendio feliz.
Acrobacias bufas…ventriloquia rara
súbita escopeta de aquella nariz
La lágrima negra de esa blanca cara.
Cleopatra sobre un coro de trompetas
saludando a las estrellas y al amor!
¡Timbales! ¡Flautines!
Latones de escándalo…absurdas cometas.
El aire abre planos y frescos jardines.
Locura, alegría, palidez, amor!
Pasa el carro lento de las odaliscas,
La comparsa blanca, la del verde humor,
pasa la comparsa de las Diez Franciscas
el carro tremendo del Emperador!
Reinas y payasos,
-por el aire vuela un bastón colorado-
los pierrots que enredan la luna en sus pasos,
tambores de Oriente de golpe encantado,
y saltos de espejos y noches y frutas.
Ya llegan los negros del baile sensual
con piernas de títeres y risas de luna
que se duermen sobre el bombo tropical;
los negros fantástico e imaginativos
que se dramatizan en vagos y vivos
saludos de monos y gestos de chivos
que se ríen por la médula espinal.
Trae un auto una súbita bandeja de ángeles
y tras otro, Walkiria de veloces cabellos de papel
cruza uno que se aleja tirando los divinos
cascabeles de un lunático arlequín.
Pasa la astronómica murga de los chinos
-qué triste, adelante, va el pálido y dulce mandarín!
Me corta el jinete

de una serpentina con su duende azul!
(Cuidado con esa niña que es como un juguete
defendiendo sus alas de tul)
Y el corso levanta la noche en sus brazos dorados.
Largo trópico de música por la calle popular.
Atrás turbia pena de dientes morados,
esta es mi pirueta, mi nariz, mi andar!
Y miro esa casa:
el balcón se ríe con barbas de cintas y velos,
suena una ventana…un antifaz pasa…
y yo soñé que es ella que está con los otros
bailando a esa música de agua y violoncellos…
Las estrellas corren en sus bicicletas
plateadas y azules por el "boulevard"
saltan, como rosas, tristes morisquetas,
y yo ya estoy loco de nunca alcanzar
la boca fantástica de ese antifaz fino
que toda la noche me hizo palpitar.
Pero en esa esquina
cuatro dominós se han quedado quietos,
y yo tengo miedo en aquella esquina
de los dominós parados y quietos.
¡Vamos Ana!
¡Dame el brazo Margarita!
En esa casa hay un baile que parece la campana
de una locura infinita!
Préndete, a mi, Josefina!
en mis barbas coloradas llevo el circo del amor!
Yo sé lo que no te ha dicho esa loca serpentina
que en tu moño fue durmiéndose como si fuera una flor.
Pero el Corso pasa…
¡Pasa!
¡Trampolín para el acróbata lívido del corazón!
¡Regatas de aguas, de cintas, de payasos y mujeres
con sus viñas de alegría y sus bocas de ilusión!
Pasa el corso…
Pasa…pasa…!
Y ya la calle está sola…por el suelo hay una máscara
perdida
Y es tan grave este último payaso que se mete en esa casa
de
una sola ventanita encendida!
Y otra vez el Corso rompe en su camino
La nube de gritos que es su cascabel!
¡Los osos! Las hadas…la reina…el bandido…

son todos los cuentos que a la calle han salido
fabulosamente libres de sus casas de papel...!
Llega la volanta de las colombinas
-a la rubia de la risa yo le tiro esta flor-
Se va la volanta de las colombinas.
Y serenata de serpentinas
van llamándola en la calle con sus flautas de color!
Perdidos, antiguos, plateados, fragantes
pedazos de música me dan su temblor.
-Hay baile en aquellos balcones distantes-
Y yo sé que es ella la de aquellos guantes
que tras el cristal da su espalda en una
disolución de luna
que sobre el negro corpiño le abre su flor.
Pasa el Corso con su río
que va a perderse a la luna con su estrépito triunfal.
Y en la ciudad que se queda como un gran teatro vacío
yo siento que el corazón mío
se pasea como un gato solitario y fantasmal.
¡Se va el Corso! Se va el ruido
Pero yo me cuelgo, mágico, a tu luz y tus amores
Carnaval!
¡Salud inmensa aventura de las aguas y las flores
que nos dejan las cabezas como trompos de colores
dando vuelvas, vueltas, vueltas
en tu mano de cristal.

Poem Six

Letter from my Mother

A letter that I was waiting for in fear
a letter I've scarcely
read, distracted by the dinning room.
This letter from mother...the one that only
makes me tremble,
turn pale and yell...
Postman! How late did you come today!
With his deafness of alcohol he was going to poison me.
This letter from her...letter that I waited for!
A sudden happiness filled my heart!
And with a few rare doubts in which I'll die
alone and pale with, as a thief.
A letter from my mother that already I have forgotten,
in which she only sends me orders
ay! Letters that so many times have saved me,
this time...cannot, forgive me so?

Spanish Version

CARTA DE MI MADRE

Carta que esperaba antes con temblor
carta que ahora apenas
leo distraído por el comedor.
Carta de ella...la carta que solo
ya me hace temblar
palidecer o gritar...
¡Cartero! ¡Qué tarde llegaste hoy día!
Con su sordo alcohol me iba a envenenar.
Carta de ella... ¡Carta que ya solo espero!
¡Alegrías súbitas en mi corazón!
O unas dudas raras con las que me muero
Solitario y pálido como un ladrón.

44

Carta de mi madre que ya te he olvidado
por la que ella solo me puede mandar
¡Ay! Carta que tantas veces me has salvado,
esta vez…¿No me puedes perdonar?

Poem Seven

English Version

Zuray Zurita's Serenade

It has eyelids, the moon, and my agony
I came as a madman from the sea of dreaming.
I got lost at a silent port, where the day
was weary of waiting.

Zuray Zurita
don't you hear me weeping?
I had gone to the sea with sails and colors…
for on land I was tired of fighting…
a stubborn seeker's dream
hurting from my ways and throbs,
I wanted to wait for her.

Zuray Zurita
don't you hear me weeping?

And I said to the dove and to the star:
my heart wants to find her,
waning of songs I departed after her
speechless she is, more so than death, and so beautiful!
and she is finer than the deep.

Zuray Zurita
don't you hear me weeping?

Bitterness, has stained me
demanding and slaying years have taught me to forget…
Blue moon overhead: such madness,
and to all the waves of the sea, my fast rambler 's cape.

Zuray Zurita
don't you hear me weeping?

And I said to her, I come a stranger,
you do not remember me,
drop by drop I gave my blood, all these years…
I am sightless for calling…

Zuray Zurita
don't you hear me weeping?
The sky has a bell
and a garden the sea
headlines fill the morning like flags,
I saw her...yet my soul could not reach her.

Zuray Zurita
don't you hear me weeping?

I have seen in souls and upper bodies
of a scorpion's drill and strike...
I have seen homes disengaged
and to the clowns with their colors, the moon is their roof
 here they give a stellar jump.

Zuray Zurita
don't you hear me weeping?

With the harp of the dawn I was getting myself to walk...
lying, while in a melancholy laziness
a slow worm was killing me day by day
and my eyes got lost in the stars and the sea.

Zuray Zurita
don't you hear me weeping?

Spanish Version

Serenata de Zuray Zurita

Tiene párpados de luna mi agonía
De la mar yo vine loco de soñar.
Me perdí en un puerto mudo donde el día
estaba muerto de esperar
Zuray Zurita
¿no me oyes llorar?
A la mar me fui con vela de colores...
de la tierra estaba sucio de luchar...
Tercos sueños cazadores
Dolorido de caminos y tambores,
yo la quería esperar.

Zuray Zurita
¿no me oyes llorar?
Y le dije a la paloma y a la estrella:
mi corazón la quiere encontrar,
moribundo de canciones voy tras ella
y es más muda que la muerte, ¡y es tan bella!
y es más fina que la mar.
Zuray Zurita
¿no me oyes llorar?
Me ha manchado la amargura
años arduos y asesinos me han enseñado a olvidar...
Luna azul de mi sombrero: la locura,
y mi capa de andarín: todas las olas del mar.
Zuray Zurita
¿no me oyes llorar?
Y le dije vengo extraño,
no me puedes recordar,
gota a gota di mi sangre todo el año...
estoy ciego de llamar...
Zuray Zurita
¿no me oyes llorar?
Tiene el cielo una campana
y un jardín tiene la mar.
Volanta de cintas llena de mañana,
la vi...y no la pudo mi alma alcanzar.
Zuray Zurita
¿no me oyes llorar?
Yo he visto en almas y pechos
a un alacrán perforar...
yo he visto hogares deshechos
y a payasos de colores que a la luna de los techos
daban un brinco estelar.
Zuray Zurita
¿no me oyes llorar?
Con el arpa de la aurora me ponía a caminar...
Pérfida languidez de la melancolía
me iba una seda lenta matando día a día
y mis ojos se perdieron en las estrellas del mar.
Zuray Zurita
¿no me oyes llorar?

Additional poems by:

Juan Parra del Riego

(Poems extracted in Spanish from the book: "Mañana con el Alba Obra Poética Completa", 1994 Translated by: Dennis L. Siluk, Ed.D, and Rosa Peñaloza de Siluk

Poem Eight

English Version

The Vidalita

They are three romantic souls: the thoughtful moon,
the Creole that sings since evening
and the warm guitar that trembles from on high
sitting on its lap such as a woman.

And that is when sprouts the verse that captivates,
as of two sad eyes that are placed to see
the measure of that slow sensitive music
that is daybreak, and weeping and love that makes
      another come back...

Because the grief of race that the *Vidalita* has,
has something that dies and something that resurrects
in the large landscapes of the meadows with the moon

that saw, trembling, to the last wandering guitarist
getting down from the horse with the guitar before a
window where there was the death and the love.

La Vidalita

Son tres almas románticas: la luna pensativa,
el criollo que canta desde el atardecer
y la guitarra cálida que tiembla desde arriba
y se sienta en sus faldas tal como una mujer.

Y es cuando brota entonces la copla que cautiva
como dos ojos tristes que se ponen a ver
al compás de esa lenta música sensitiva
que es madrugada, y llanto, y amor que hace volver...

Porque el dolor de raza que hay en la vidalita
tiene algo que se muere y algo que resucita
en los paisajes largos de la pampa con luna

que vio, temblando, al último rondante payador
bajarse del caballo con la guitarra ante una
ventana donde estaban la muerte y el amor.

Poem Nine

English Version

Her Laugh

Goblins with hand bells
that came from the sea,
fresh as the moon
their hearts come out
to play...

Goblins that turn round
suddenly to the sea...

Note: Written for his wife, in the book "Blanca Luz Poemas"

Spanish Version

Su Risa

Duendes con campanillas
que venían del mar,
fresco como la luna
su corazón se salía
a jugar...

Duendes que se volvían
de repente a la mar...

Nota: Escrito para su esposa en el libro "Blanca Luz"

The Windmills

In the ravine the windmills are
the melancholy and vibrating page
that tells us of its ingenuous tradition.
Oh the windmills and its symbolic peace!

Its big rotating rotor blades
sing with its perpetual movements
a psalm of work in the deep loudness
and lyrical madness of the winds.

They are so high so as to sometimes deceive
and in the afternoon we believe that they
accompany
that large ghostly entourage.

Of clouds of mourners, in late step
that brings the corpse
to the unexplained crypt of the sunset

Spanish Version

Los Molinos

En el Barranco los molinos son
la página vibrante y melancólica
que nos dice su ingenua tradición.
¡Oh los molinos y su paz simbólica!

Sus grandes mariposas giradoras
cantan con sus perennes movimientos
un salmo de trabajo en las sonoras
y líricas locuras de los vientos.

Son tan altos que a veces engañan
y en las tardes creemos que acompañan
ese largo cortejo fantasmal.

De nubes de doliente y tardo paso
que lleva el cadáver vesperal
al mágico sepulcro del ocaso.

Poem Eleven

English Version

The Park

I don't know what evocative sadness
the flowery park of Barranco has,
that keeps under its dreamy shade
a recollection of love on each bench.

A fiesta of crystalline flutes
in the morning makes happy its branches,
and in the languid hours of the evening
stir up innocent laughs.

But in the discreet and opportune peace
of the romantic nights of the moon
is sadder, more alone, more quiet ...

And under a protector jacaranda
I do not know who, sitting in a bench
by the shadow, is asking if she will come.

Spanish Version

El Parque

Yo no sé qué tristeza evocadora
tiene el florido parque de Barranco,
que guarda ante su sombra soñadora
un recuerdo de amor en cada banco.

Una fiesta de flautas cristalinas
por la mañana alegra sus ramadas,
y en las lánguidas horas vespertinas
la alborotan ingenuas carcajadas.

Pero en la paz discreta y oportuna
de las noches románticas de la luna
es más triste, más sola, más callada...

Y bajo un protector jacarandá
no sé quién en algún banco sentado
se pregunta en la sombra si vendrá.

Poem Twelve

Far

Head of my mother that I do not kiss
since clashed ten years already,
Head with grey hair that I have never forgotten,
a sleeping moon in my heart.

I think in the years that are lost...
with golden wings, of silver and music
I went to life
It was like the sun!

Chest full of confused hatred,
tighten brow of aching
intoxicating memories
Where will I go today?

Head, with grey hair, hope you never find out
that my heart is so black...
With your remote sweet ashes
maybe someday God will cure me.

Spanish Version

Lejos

Cabeza de mi madre que no beso
desde hace ya diez años de fragor,
cabeza cana que nunca olvido,
luna dormida en mi corazón.

Pienso en los años que se han perdido...
Con alas de oro, de plata y música
me fui a la vida
¡era como el sol!

Pecho cargado de odios confusos,
frente apretada de doloridos
vinos de recuerdos
¿a dónde iré hoy?

Cabeza cana, que nunca sepas
que está tan negro mi corazón...
Con tu remota ceniza dulce
quizá algún día me cure Dios.

†

Two Accompanying Poems:
Christmas and Kisses

By Juan Parra del Riego
Translated by Rosa Peñaloza de Siluk & Edited by D. L. Siluk,
Poet Laureate

Paris, as Juan Parra del Riego most likely saw it. I was there four times myself, and it is perhaps one of the few places on earth poets, artists, and novelists care to see and experience, at least once in a life time, a cultural pilgrimage of sorts. When Juan Parra del Riego was there, he ended up becoming broke, and had to borrow money to get back home; but to my understanding, it was a highlight for his life; as it was for me, and most other artists. Dlsiluk

▼

English Version

Magic Christmas Eve!
(Two Fragments)

It was in Lima, the golden colonial city...
Do you remember, oh, mother, of the Christmas Eve night
    so sentimental?
     I still look at the dinner,
the silver thread that rains from the tree.
    God was in the house
the great sidekick of that happiness.
     ...

Notes: Information, and poetic fragments taken from the book, "PROSA (1943, Uruguay)"

Spanish Version

¡Noche Buena Mágica!

Era en Lima, la áurea ciudad colonial...
Te acuerdas, oh, madre, de la Nochebuena
    tan sentimental?
    Yo aun miro la cena,
los hilos de plata que el árbol llovía.
    Dios era en la casa
el buen compañero de aquella alegría.
    ...

Nota: Información, y fragmentos poéticos tomados del libro (1943, Uruguay)"

"Kisses"
(Madness before death: with commentary notes)

Note: All poems for this book were selected (or chosen with careful review) in August of 2007, except for "Kisses," chosen, and added to this selection in, October, of 2008 for its extraordinary content, intensity, and external effects.

English Version

Kisses

Sounds of doves kissing under the moon
you have left in my mouth.
Honeycombs with delirious and wild happiness
you have left in my mouth.
Red and pure hearts of children
you have left in my mouth.
Fields with its happiness of goats and bells
you have left in my mouth.
Your dreadful and blue paleness like my death

you have left in my mouth.

Notes: this extraordinary work (poem) "Kisses" chronicles the ensuing death march; he, Juan Parra del Riego was slowly undergoing, and may have been written prior to his last breaths. Much of his poetry was written the last year of his life (1925), and it clearly radiates out in this poem, "Kisses."

In "Kisses" Juan Parra del Riego takes us through some painful moments, his increasingly strained body, and mind, devastatingly brings us into its madness itself. The reader is drawn into his intensity, that his insanity becomes completely real and even rational, as if going to a good movie. He writes—unknowing perhaps, the tragedy of life—the pure truth, if not for some (and surely for me), the happiness and madness in life itself, without pretense, before death. He talks to life itself, as if it was his mistress.

Written for his wife, in the book "Blanca Luz"

Besos
Por Juan Parra del Riego

Sonidos de palomas besándose a la luna
me has dejado en la boca.
Panales de alegría delirante y salvaje
me has dejado en la boca.
Corazones de niños colorados y puros
me has dejado en la boca.
Campo con su alegría de chivos y campanas
me has dejado en la boca.
Tu palidez terrible y azul como mi muerte
me has dejado en la boca.

The following poem is a tribute to
Juan Parra del Riego's poem, 'Kisses'

by Dïsïluk

English Version

Two Pigeons Kissing

Two pigeons in the morning—
November sun
sitting on a tree-branch,
kissing outside my window…
(as if no one's around);
looking here and there!
The blue-headed one, pecking
    at its wings….

(I'm thinking, staring—:
can life be so simple?)

No: 2516 (11-15-2008), written in:
El Tambo, Huancayo, Peru (a tribute to Juan Parra del Riego)

Spanish Version

Dos Pichones Besándose

¡Dos pichones en la mañana—
en el sol de noviembre
sentados en una rama del árbol,
están besándose afuera de mi ventana…
(como si nadie estuviera alrededor);
mirando aquí y allá!
El de la cabeza azul, picoteándose
    sus alas…

(Mirando fijamente, estoy pensando—:
¿Puede la vida ser tan simple?)

Nro. 2516 (15-Noviembre-2008), escrito en:
El Tambo, Huancayo, Perú (un homenaje a Juan Parra del Riego)

♦

Overview of:
The Life and Times of Blanca Luz Brum
(Wife of Juan Parra del Riego)

By Dennis L. Siluk

Blanca Luz. Montevideo. 1924

Blanca Luz Brum, 1924 (18-years old)
Born 1905, died 1985 (80-years old)
Married Juan Parra del Riego, in 1925,
Juan Parra died that same year at the age of thirty-one
from tuberculosis.

There is something relevant, to Blanca Luz Brum's long life, and short marriage to Juan Parra del Riego, in many ways Blanca lived a more exciting life than he, but then she lived pert near fifty-years longer than he. But to know the poet (Juan Parra...), it is wise to know his wife of perhaps less than a year. Juan Parra died five days after Blanca gave birth to his one and only son; and it has been said, in the last hour before he died, he was writing a poem: a dedicated poet, and romantic for sure.

She, Blanca was born in Pan de Azucar, and died in Chile, and was a writer as well as revolutionary, likened to her Employer, Evita Peron, whom she was secretary for.

She became well known throughout South America within her lifetime, having friendships with many artists, writers and poets, as well as

63

politicians; among some was Pablo Neruda, who was one year older than her, and Huidobro, as well as other legendary writers; a woman of and for culture. She spent a number of her later years, on the South Pacific island, of 'Robinson Crusoe.'

In her lifetime, she married many times, and had many lovers, yet she had humble beginnings. Juan Parra met her at a convent, while visiting it one day with a friend. It would seem it didn't take long for them to get acquainted (along with a few of those motorcycle rides he gave her), and shortly thereafter married. It was heard that he said, "My motorbike is happy like the sun," meaning, to carry him and her together on it, and it would seem at this juncture he had finished his motion poem, of a motorcycle, and wish for her to read it.

After the death of her husband, she went to Peru to visit Juan Parra's family, and the rest is history which can be discovered in part, by reading Hugo Achugar's book, "False Memories: Blanca Luz Brum" 2001, by Trilce Editions; she was a lovely lady, and a woman of her times, a scholar, revolutionary, writer, traveler and to my understanding, a good wife to Juan Parra, and loving mother to her their son.

Sinopsis de:
La Vida y Tiempos de Blanca Luz Brum
(Esposa de Juan Parra del Riego)

Por Dennis L. Siluk

En la foto aparece:
Blanca Luz Brum, 1924 (18 años de edad)
Nació en 1905 y murió en 1985 a los ochenta años de edad.
Casada con Juan Parra del Riego en 1925,
Juan murió el mismo año a los treintiún años de edad de tuberculosis.

Hay algo importante en la larga vida de Blanca Luz Brum y su corto matrimonio con Juan Parra del Riego; ella, en muchos sentidos vivió una vida más emocionante que la de Juan, y es que ella vivió cerca de cincuenta años más que él. Pero para conocer al poeta (Juan Parra del Riego) es sensato conocer a su esposa de menos de un año talvez. Juan Parra del riego murió cinco días después que Blanca Luz diera a luz a su único hijo; y se ha dicho, que en las últimas horas antes de morir, él estaba escribiendo un poema: un poeta dedicado y romántico él era por seguro.

Ella, Blanca Luz nació en Pan de Azúcar y murió en Chile y era escritora así como también revolucionaria, similar a su empleador, Perón, de quien ella era su secretaria de prensa.

Blanca Luz se hizo conocida en toda Sudamérica durante su existencia, habiendo tenido amistad con muchos artistas, escritores y poetas, así como también políticos; entre algunos de ellos estaban Pablo Neruda, quien era un año mayor que ella, Huidobro, así como también otros escritores famosos; era una mujer culta y por la cultura. Ella vivió varios años en la Isla de Robinson Crusoe en el Pacífico sur.

Durante su vida ella se casó varias veces así como tuvo muchos amantes, sin embargo ella tuvo unos comienzos humildes. Juan Parra del Riego la conoció en un convento mientras un día él visitaba este con un amigo. Parecería que no tomó mucho tiempo para que ellos se conocieran (junto con unos cuantos viajes en motocicleta que él le daba), y poco tiempo después de esto ellos se casaron. Se dice que él le decía, "Mi motocicleta está feliz como el sol", queriendo decir, de llevarle a él y a ella juntos, y parecería que a este punto él ya había acabado de escribir su "Polirritmo de la Motocicleta" y deseaba que ella lo leyera.

Después de la muerte de su esposo, Juan Parra del Riego, ella fue a Perú a visitar a la familia de él, y el resto de esta historia puede ser descubierta en parte leyendo el libro de Hugo Achugar llamado "Falsas Memorias de Blanca Luz Brum" del 2001 by Ediciones Trilce. Ella era una encantadora dama y una mujer de su tiempo, una erudita, revolucionaria, escritora, viajera, y a mi entendimiento, una buena esposa de Juan Parra del Riego y madre cariñosa de su hijo.

End to the Book "Juan Parra del Riego"

End Poem
By Dennis L. Siluk

Death Passed Me Once
(In the Valley of Days)

Death returns: it found no resting place,
I saw it in flight last night—(it passed me once,
overhead) beneath the last sparks of twilight—!

Death has wings, you know, I saw it descend,
it glides through the valley of days, in peacefulness…
yet—its tail leaves shadows of grief, and pain,
to return at dawn, blue-bellied full—,
as if it had swallowed a whale whole.

Death, is always hungry it seems, and has an
invisible web nearby, always waiting, waiting,
likened to a spider waiting for a fly!

Poema Final
Por Dennis L. Siluk

La Muerte me Sobrepasó una Vez
(En el Valle de la Vida)

¡La muerte vuelve: esta no encontró un lugar para descansar,
la vi en vuelo, anoche—(esta me sobrepasó una vez)
debajo de las últimas chispas del crepúsculo—!

La muerte tiene alas, tú sabes, la vi descender,
esta se desliza a través del valle de la vida, en sosiego…
aunque—su cola deja sombras de aflicción, y dolor,
para volver al amanecer, estómago azul lleno—,
como si se hubiera tragado una ballena entera.

¡La muerte, parece que siempre está hambrienta, y tiene
una telaraña invisible cerca, siempre esperando, esperando,
similar a una araña y una mosca!

Complimentary Poems

English Version

I Simply Write
by Poet Apolinario Mayta Inga
(Stanza one of three)
Translated and Edited by Dennis and Rosa Siluk

It is not a drama:
the afternoon
coming out to the
bank of the river.
Calling
your name to the bed of the river grass
Absent your smile.
A flock of white birds
(overhead) with their guitar.
The world falling apart.
Woman, and you woman
losing the dream of the man,
in your womb.
…

Simplemente Escribo

Por el Poeta Apolinario Mayta Inga
(Primera estrofa de tres)

No es drama:
La tarde
saliéndose a la
ribera del río.
Llamándome
tu nombre al juncal.
Ausente tu sonrisa.
Parvadas de aves blancas
con su guitarra.
El mundo desbarrancándose.
Mujer, y tú mujer
perdiendo el sueño del hombre,
en tu vientre.
...

♦

"In the Nick of Time"
By Poet Cindy White (8-8-2006)
Translated and Edited by Dennis and Rosa Siluk

I met Dennis (Siluk) at B&N
Café—a decent place to
write and draw. To
set one's creative juices
among the crowd. Among
the roar of the blender that
would wind up words for
a poet—any poet.

Dennis is an inspiration,
for this lowly poet, as
I sit in the same B/N
café without him, thinking
of his new life in Peru.
Thinking I might catch
his spirit, his muse and
sprout my words.

It was an honour; still
is an honour to sit
in this space, where
one poet met another poet
in the nick of time.

Spanish Version

"Justo a Tiempo"
Por la Poetisa Cindy White
Traducido y Editado por:
Dennis L. Siluk y Rosa Peñaloza de Siluk

Conocí a Dennis (Siluk) en el
Café de Barnes y Noble—
un lugar decente para
escribir y dibujar. Para
poner los creativos zumos de uno
entre la multitud. Entre
el estruendo de la licuadora que

finalizaría las palabras para
un poeta—cualquier poeta.

Dennis es una inspiración
para esta poetisa modesta, mientras
me siento en el mismo café de
Barnes y Noble sin él, pensando
en su nueva vida en Perú.
Pensando talvez pueda coger
su espíritu, su meditar y
hacer brotar mis palabras.

Fue un honor; todavía
es un honor sentarme
en este lugar, donde
un poeta conoció a otro poeta
justo a tiempo.

♦

CITY OF HUANCAYO

By Cesar Gamarra Berrocal
Translated by Rosa Peñaloza de Siluk
Edited by Dennis L. Siluk

What to do when the time
accumulates in my eyes.
Fig-tree and stories
and I go through the streets
without any direction:
I lost my notebook
and it comes to me any name
and I start writing:
"When I travel I acquire some capacity of
communication
          with my world"
and I do not open *Udana*.
Buda behind the counter
and I do not know what is the time
there is only
the wind / the dust and a plaza.

CIUDAD DE HUANCAYO
Por César Gamarra Berrocal
(Poeta Peruano y Comentarista de Televisión)

Qué hacer cuando el tiempo
se acumula en mis ojos.
Higuera e historias
y voy atravesando calles
sin ningún sentido:

perdí mi libreta de apuntes
y me viene cualquier nombre
y empiezo a escribir:
"Cuando viajo adquiero cierta capacidad de
comunicación
              con mi mundo"
y no abro Udana.
Buda detrás del mostrador
y no sé qué es el tiempo
sólo hay
el viento / el polvo y una plaza.

The Color of Life

Written by Jaime Bravo Gaspar
(Written in September, 2008)
Translated and edited by: Dennis L. Siluk, Ed.D.,
and Rosa Peñaloza de Siluk

I know the horrors of a paralyzing midnight
in lonely parks,
of the inconveniencies that from there
return as seer-cats
to settle on colorless landscapes
inside of photographs in sepia,
but not the colors that reflect
the skies that rest in her eyes;
them, they are the guilty,
that what one sees amongst the debris
returns to be perfumed
and again I am consoled with a frail hug
from a distorted light in a rainbow,
with dilated pupils,
ready to weep a tear
onto a leaf of the eucalyptus
a drop, one drop of abandoned dew
onto the pink cheek, of my desired woman.

Spanish Version

El Color de la Vida

Por Jaime Bravo Gaspar

Conozco los horrores de la medianoche
entumecida en parques solitarios,
de las incomodidades que de allá
retornan como gatos agoreros
a posarse en paisajes monocromáticos
dentro de fotografías en sepia,

mas no de los colores que reflejan
los cielos y que descansan en sus ojos,
ellos, son los culpables
de que lo que uno mira entre escombros
vuelvan a estar perfumados,
y otra vez ser consolado con un frágil abrazo
de una luz descompuesta en un arco iris,
o en las pupilas dilatadas,
prestos para derramar una gota de lágrima
en una hoja de eucalipto
o en una gota de rocío abandonada
en la mejilla rosada de mi deseada mujer.

The Long Glimpse
By Dr. Dennis L. Siluk, Ed.D.

From the arch of the doorway
She'd look my way, into the garage, at me—
as I readied my automobile to go someplace;
She'd be looking-steadfast
I'd open my car door a bit, ask:
    "Why you staring? (at me)"
    "No reason," she'd reply, smiling.
Then with a tinge of hesitation
she summoned up, and said (at 82):
softly, in an almost whisper "You…."
((as if she had remembered the day I
    was born) (almost in a trance.))
And I'd for the life of me—
not know why; I know now though, she was
simply getting a long glimpse before
she died (for she died shortly after).
I guess, she was really saying goodbye,
saying goodbye with a long glimpse
to last between now and then,
when we'd meet again.

No: 1947 8-24-2007. Dedicated to: Elsie T. Siluk

El Vistazo Largo
Por Dr. Dennis L. Siluk

Desde el marco de la puerta,
Ella miraría mi camino, en el garaje, a mí—
Mientras yo alistaba mi carro para ir a algún lugar;
Ella estaría mirando persistentemente,
Yo abriría un poco la puerta de mi carro,
preguntaría:
    "¿Por qué me miras fijamente?"

"Ninguna razón", ella contestaría, sonriendo.
Entonces con un poquito de vacilación
ella se armaría de valor y diría (a sus 82 años),
suavemente, casi en un suspiro: "A ti..."
((como si ella hubiera recordado el día
    en que nací) (casi en un trance)).
Y yo, por mi vida—
no sabría por qué, aunque ahora lo sé; ella estaba
simplemente echando un largo vistazo antes
de morir (ya que ella murió poco después).
Pienso, que ella realmente se estaba despidiendo,
diciendo ¡adiós! con un largo vistazo
para perdurar entre ahora y entonces,
cuando nos encontremos de nuevo.

1947 24-Agosto-2007. Dedicado a Elsie T. Siluk.

Books by the Author

Out of Print

The Other Door, Volume I   *[1981] ((poetry) (poems written in 1960s &
'70s))*
The Tale of Willie the Humpback Whale |1982| (chapbook)
The Tale of Freddy the Foolish Frog ((1982) (chapbook))
The Tale of Teddy and His Magical Plant ((1983) (chapbook))
The Tale of the Little Rose's Smile ((1983) (chapbook))
The Tale of Alexi's Mysterious Pot ((1984) (chapbook))
Two Modern Short Stories of Immigrant life |1984| (chapbook)
The Safe Child/the Unsafe Child |1985| (for teachers, of Minnesota
Schools)

Presently In Print

The Last Trumpet and the Woodbridge Demon (2002) Visions
Angelic Renegades & Raphaim Giants (2002) Visions

Tales of the Tiamat |trilogy|

Tiamat, Mother of Demon   I (2002)
Gwyllion, Daughter of the Tiamat   II (2002)
Revenge of the Tiamat III ((2002) (in English and Spanish))

Every day's Adventure (2002) Pot Luck
Islam, In Search of Satan's Rib (2002) Opinion

The Addiction Books of D.L. Siluk:

A Path to Sobriety (2002)
A Path to Relapse Prevention (2003)
Aftercare: Chemical Dependency Recovery (2004)

Autobiographical

A Romance in Augsburg   I "2003)
Romancing San Francisco   II   (2003)
Where the Birds Don't Sing   III (2003)
Stay Down, Old Abram   IV (2004)
Chasing the Sun |Travels of D.L Siluk| (2002)

Romance and Tragedy:

The Rape of Angelina of Glastonbury 1199 AD (2002) Novelette
Perhaps it's Love (Minnesota to Seattle)   2004 Novel
Cold Kindness (Dieburg, Germany)   2005   Novelette

The Suspense short stories, Novels and Novelettes:

Death on Demand |Seven Suspenseful Short Stories| 2003 Vol: I
Dracula's Ghost |And other Peculiar stories| 2003 Vol: II
The Jumping Serpents of Bosnia
(and other Suspenseful, Eldritch-writings) 2008 Vol: III
 The Mumbler |psychological| 2003 (Novel)

After Eve [a prehistoric adventure] (2004) Novel
Mantic ore: Day of the Beast ((2002) (Novelette)) supernatural

The Poetry of D.L. Siluk:

The Other Door (Poems- Volume I, 1981)
Willie the Humpback Whale (poetic tale)
(1982; 1983, 2008, four printings (in Spanish & English)
Sirens [Poems-Volume II, 2003] *(poetry from the 50s thru the '90s)*
The Macabre Poems [Poems-Volume III, 2004]
Last Autumn and Winter [Minnesota poems, 2006]
Spell of the Andes [2005] *English and Spanish*
Peruvian Poems [2005] *English and Spanish*
Poetic Images out of Peru [And other poems, 2006] *In English and Spanish*
The Magic of the Avelinos (Mantaro Valley, book One; 2006) *English and Spanish*
The Road to Unishcoto (Mantaro Valley, Book Two, 2007) *English and Spanish*
The Poetry of Stone Forest (Cerro de Pasco, 2007) *English and Spanish*

> *The Selected Translated Poetry of Juan Parra del Riego (by D.L. Siluk, 2009)*
> *Days without Women ((autobiographical sketches) (2010))*
> *Old Josh, in Poor Black ((A Novel in Sketches of the Old South) (2010))*

Juan Parra del Riego (King of the Peruvian Poets) his poetry describes and interweaves the thorny parts of his life with love, tenderness, rowdiness, hunger, restlessness, and compassion. The master of Polirritmo in the time of Modernism in poetry. He lived only until his 31st birthday. Born in Huancayo, Peru, he moved to Uruguay, where he started his own movement, married Blanca Luz Brum, whom he had one child with. A first time translation of a Great poet.

Included in the book are four complimentary poems by other poets; and tributes by the author, for Juan Parra del Riego. The book has been a seventeen-month project by the author and his wife.

From one of the top 100-reviewers, at Amazon Books, International (largest bookseller in the world), by Robert C. Ross, the list author says (reference to the book: "Peruvian Poems"): "Dennis L. Siluk is enormously prolific and very well travelled…. The poems are based on places and experiences in Peru, written in both English and Spanish, and provide a fascinating backdrop in preparation for a trip to Peru." (1-1-2009) Also this book was shown on National Television by Cesar Hildebrandt, considered '…a very important book for Peruvian Culture.'

About the Author

This is Dennis' 39th book, 12th in Poetry. He lives in Minnesota and Peru with his wife, Rosa. He has a worldwide audience, and has traveled extensively. Back picture is of the author at the Barnes and Nobel bookstore, February, 2006, Har Mar Mall, Roseville, Minnesota, doing a book signing.

Printed in the United States
by Baker & Taylor Publisher Services